a pocket full of wisdom

by Bernice Angoh

First Printing, 2022
Publisher: www.paperheartbook.com

Dedicated to you, oh wanderer!

As you meditate daily on each entry
May the words unlock answers to your questions
May each feeling awaken & heal the child within you
May life present you with knowing and trust
that you are loved, and you are safe in this vast unknown

Bernice Angoh

"Make yourself seen and heard."

"I want to know you" said I to Love,

Love: "Do you not hear my constant song of your heartbeat,

Do you not taste me as I swell up in you and flows down your cheeks?

Do you not see the manifestations of my strength when you soar?

Do you not smell the fragrance of me in the things that you love?

Do you not feel me when you exhale against your skin…"

i am

Don't be so wrapped up in a world of "staying positive" all the time
that you deny yourself the opportunity to feel anything else.

toxic positivity

Bernice Angoh

If we can all agree that a butterfly was once a crawling caterpillar
Or that a seed needs to be buried deep into the soil to die
and split open to sprout into a plant
Then pain, discomfort and darkness are not a thing for us to be afraid of,
to avoid or to resist
They are our friends with messages for us

metamorphosis

A Pocket Full of Wisdom

When I allow myself to be seduced by the calling of my soul
I find that not only am I beautiful just the way I am,
Everything I come across reveals its own beauty to me

self-awareness

Do not disappoint yourself in the pursuit
of making everyone else happy
Break your own record
So long as you are authentic,
Go ahead and "disappoint" as many people as possible!

authenticity

Whenever pain shows up,
I say to myself,
"Oh, look, my healing has come!"

h*ealing*

You can always measure your growth
by the ease with which you
let things go.

self-growth

You must be quiet loud enough
to hear your soul speak

stillness

Bernice Angoh

Gratitude is the awareness
that what is given in each moment is enough

contentment

A Pocket Full of Wisdom

Bernice Angoh

At times,
the universe will allow you to experience it all
in order for you not to be moved by it anymore

pain, rejection, disappointment

A Pocket Full of Wisdom

Where there is silence
there is peace
Only words have the
capability
to create chaos

sounds of silence

A Pocket Full of Wisdom

Bernice Angoh

Be so absorbed in the present moment
that you have no use for hope

h*ope-less*

A Pocket Full of Wisdom

Bernice Angoh

Everything in life
is teaching us to R.E.S.T
R.emember E.verything'S T.ransient

DeepREST

A Pocket Full of Wisdom

Bernice Angoh

I am powerful...
because I love

true power

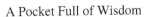

A Pocket Full of Wisdom

There are those who SAY, "I love you."
And then there are those who DO "I love you."
Know the difference

love is a verb

Bernice Angoh

Let your heart be the gardener of your mind

soul gardening

A Pocket Full of Wisdom

Bernice Angoh

Sometimes the enemy is us wearing our pain
out in the sun

the enemy within

A Pocket Full of Wisdom

Bernice Angoh

The bravest and most sacred thing you can ever do
is to be unapologetically YOU

YOU-nique

A Pocket Full of Wisdom

Bernice Angoh

.

Do not be afraid of your 'nakedness'
truth never needs a garment

truth, vulnerability

A Pocket Full of Wisdom

I love you is not a promise for forever
it is a promise of kindness
Not only kindness to the other but
kindness to oneself,
It says:
I have opened the flood gates of my heart to you
but I decide what comes and goes
And because I love myself too
it is still love if I choose to let go

self-love

Until the seduction of the unknown becomes
more desirable than the fear of it,
man will never know true freedom

freedom

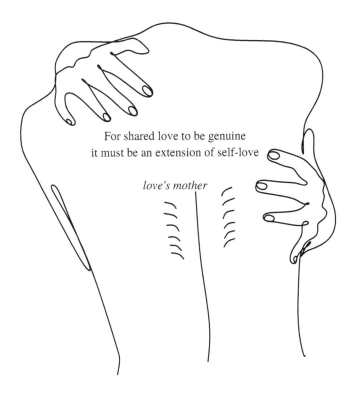

For shared love to be genuine
it must be an extension of self-love

love's mother

Bernice Angoh

To love is to go beyond understanding

go *beyond your beliefs*

A Pocket Full of Wisdom

A time will come when your compassion for self
will be higher than judgement
And in your compassion
you will discover the heaven you've always dreamed of
for yourself and for all of humankind

be gentle with yourself

Bernice Angoh

Your smile is an unwritten love letter

smile often

A Pocket Full of Wisdom

Bernice Angoh

There is no love like surrender

flow

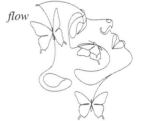

A Pocket Full of Wisdom

Bernice Angoh

Each day life gives us a free ticket
to the ultimate cosmic adventure

remain childlike

A Pocket Full of Wisdom

Be not afraid of the dark
it is where you shine the most
don't you know that darkness is the backdrop
to your spotlight?

take the stage

When pain shows up at your doorstep
remember, she's merely there
to point the way

the guide

Bernice Angoh

Habit is the bridge on which man walks
to where he sees himself to be

habit

A Pocket Full of Wisdom

Bernice Angoh

The only time humanity will ever know peace
is when we remember that
we are the saviors we seek

we are gods

A Pocket Full of Wisdom

If you only hold on to your highs
and disregard the beauty of your lows
you'd make a lousy wave
be brave, take a dive
it is the oscillations that gives
the ocean its beauty

deep dive ✧

Bernice Angoh

Sometimes you miss the people you know
because their masks are more important to them
than bearing reality

masqueraders

A Pocket Full of Wisdom

Don't go looking for love
you'll never find it
she is as concealed as your nose underneath your eyes
and as apparent as your reflection in the mirror

you are love

Every experience is leading you to the light
you will get there with less suffering
if you learn to relax, let go and
simply surrender

as it is

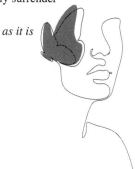

You hold the keys to all your possibilities
you alone are the dice to every probability

roll your dice

"I want to know you," said I to Love
Love: "I am the peaceful wind inside you
the magical sound of raindrops on your roof top--can you hear me call?
I am the child you once were
the laughter that brings tears to your eyes--can you feel my love?
I am the prisoner that wants to be set free
the loner who longs for a hug--can you see me reaching out?
I am the sigh that brings you joy
water running between your toes--can you taste my friendship?
I am everything that's pure
seashells giggling as they tumble towards the shore
I am your smiles, I am your blues
--can you smell my blessings in the morning dew?"

i am

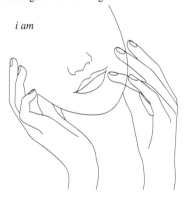

Coincidence is a word we use when
we're unable to see the inevitable succession
of our thoughts, words, and decisions

trust

Bernice Angoh

If you want to know the secret of the trinity
think thoughts, words, and actions

manifest

A Pocket Full of Wisdom

We are all guilty of theft
when we talk badly about someone behind their back.
Gossip not only steals their honor-- and ours,
it chips away at our humanity

gossip

Do not seek and ye shall find
Ask or ask not
and the answer remains to be revealed in its own time
Knock not for there is no door
Effortlessly, ah, effortlessly, life blossoms

life is a happening

A Pocket Full of Wisdom

Bernice Angoh

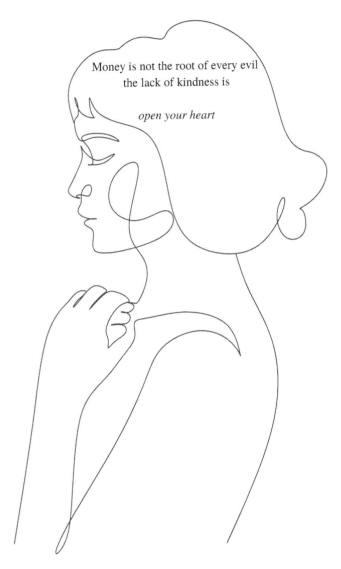

Money is not the root of every evil
the lack of kindness is

open your heart

A Pocket Full of Wisdom

A good friend is one who can take your place
on any given day
and act
in a manner that truly defines you both

friendship responsibilities

Age is an illusion that conditions
the mind to expect death
but we can all live like trees,
with no concept of time

illusive spell

Accepting breadcrumbs from relationships is a survival tactic
a sign that our inner child
is in need of gentle healing

inner child wounds

My life is not my own
it is merely borrowed to reflect this gift
called Love

on borrowed time

Bernice Angoh

Opportunity
is a stranger who simply
wants to be your friend

chance

A Pocket Full of Wisdom

Maybe,
just maybe, things that break
--in their own way--
are simply trying to multiply

h*eart-break*

Bernice Angoh

Bottled inside certain smiles
are nightmares waiting to
taste the dawn of day

resentment

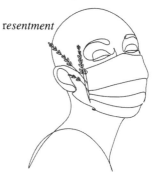

A Pocket Full of Wisdom

Bernice Angoh

The past is never the same
because we're different people when we look at it
The past with its memories, good or bad, is a prison
that will hold you captive
if you linger long enough

*Make peace with your past
or forever be in rewind*

A Pocket Full of Wisdom

In the video game of life
there's a stop button
unlike every other, it is a gracious one
begging you to stop occasionally
and recheck your bearings
While you pause, refresh, and rejuvenate
with a cool drink of reflection. Catch your breath,
drop it into some ice and crystalize your thoughts
Pause, but don't pause forever
that's just another twisted definition of quitting
You can... choose to rewind
rewind your thoughts and perspectives
have a change of heart,
readjust your belief system
rearrange them in such a way that
when you begin to play, you not only play
hard but smart...
That, my friend, is the uncomplicated
formula of success
Stop. Pause. Rewind. Play

the game of life

No one steals our dreams
it is we who choose
to give them away

the victim

It does not matter what the world
says nor what you gain
all that matters
is who you become
along the way

becoming

Bernice Angoh

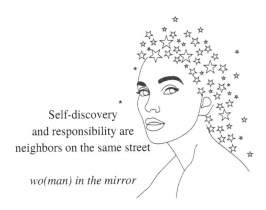

Self-discovery
and responsibility are
neighbors on the same street

wo(man) in the mirror

A Pocket Full of Wisdom

Conformity is second class
Remain first class

conditioning

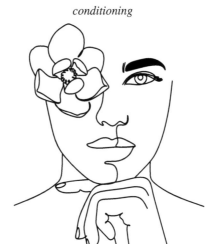

The people who don't understand you
cannot see you
And if they cannot see you
they cannot understand you
And if they don't understand you
Why do you expect them
to walk the same path as you...

sojourner

Do not discount your scars
they are sacred texts,
gospels to your inner knowing
return to your them
whenever you feel lost,
they hold the map to your journey

in-scripture

Relationships are great instigators
of growth and expansion
They're great mirrors
in which to examine the self

self-reflection

Bernice Angoh

Relationships are fantastic indicators
of self-awareness and self-love
They reveal how well
we relate to ourselves
by our choice in partners

we usually allow what we think we deserve

A Pocket Full of Wisdom

There is no "wrong person"
everyone you date
is a direct revelation of your state
of consciousness
sometimes we learn a lesson
and we move on
sometimes it was just a self-exploration
and we move on

keep it moving

A heartbreak is simply
a heart breaking open
to make room for more love

heart-break-open

Pain is a messenger
listen to what it's telling you

pain

Bernice Angoh

Suffering is a visitor
she sometimes leaves behind a gift
called resilience

suffering

A Pocket Full of Wisdom

Sorrow is the cup
that we must eventually empty
to allow room for joy and grace

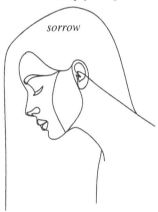

sorrow

Tears are simply an overflow of strength
they're windshield wipers of the soul

let them spill..

Love will find you
when she recognizes herself
in you

love

Bernice Angoh

A mistake
is just another word for lesson

lessons

A Pocket Full of Wisdom

Bernice Angoh

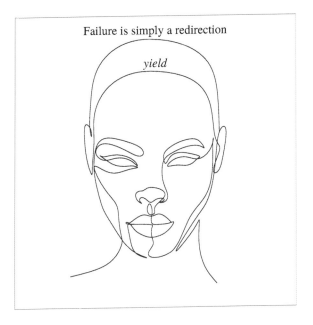

Failure is simply a redirection

yield

A Pocket Full of Wisdom

Bernice Angoh

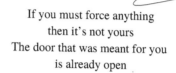

If you must force anything
then it's not yours
The door that was meant for you
is already open .

follow the path of least resistance

A Pocket Full of Wisdom

Change teaches us to break
the need to always be in control
To learn how to surrender
and to get comfortable
with the unknown

change

A rejection is usually for your protection

the beauty of "no"

A Pocket Full of Wisdom

You are the villain in someone's story
Somewhere, someone is talking about you
in the most nightmarish way
that you've talked about somebody else
It doesn't matter how good your intentions were
or how thoughtful you were
They were looking at you
through their lens of trauma and pain
Their perception of you is completely different
from what your intentions were
This alone should humble you
Most importantly
this should liberate you
from wanting to be liked or
wanting to be perfect

unshackle yourself

The discomfort that we feel
comes from either one of these two things:
Either we're trying to fit in
where we don't belong
or we're trying to remain in a place
that can no longer contain us

emancipate yourself

The change of behavior that
comes with the apology should be consistent
If it's not consistent
it wasn't an apology at all
It was just a strategy to buy time
to find a way to continue the bad behavior
without getting noticed

apology = change

When you compare
you bring upon yourself despair
When you worry
you tell yourself false stories
When you envy
you make your goals heavy
When you complain
you keep your imagination detained
And when you lie,
you entrap yourself to die

the five poisons

Sometimes, they are not a friend
Sometimes, they just want to bask in your light,
in an attempt to steal your shine
And when that doesn't happen,
they begin to find fault with you
not knowing that your glow
comes from within
And that which is from within
is inextinguishable
When that happens,
They leave bitter
But leave you better
Without them

fake friendships

Life is like a train
some people sit in the same compartment as you
but get off when their stop shows up
Sometimes, you yourself must move carts
because the one you're in
is crowded and the noise is unbearable
We don't all have the same travel plans
even though we may have a common destination
Even our itineraries are different
some people have multiple steps along the way
some people have a direct route
Sometimes you connect again
with some people who had an earlier stop
some people you notice stay with you
in the same compartment
from the start of the trip all the way to the end
When people leave your life don't be sad or angry
remember that they have their own purpose to fulfill,
and you have yours
You pay attention to your itinerary
so that you don't miss any of your stops

life's journey

Love is beyond romance
it is an infinite embrace
of growth and expansion
of grace and compassion
towards a common good

beyond romance

When you give no f*cks
life seems to not suck
when you hold your head up
life greets you with a "What's up!"
when you wholeheartedly live
it's no big deal to forgive

life's anthem

Bernice Angoh

When I began to accept
that my darkness serves me
as well as my light
all shame and guilt dissolved into
self-love
and compassion for others

hello darkness, my old friend

A Pocket Full of Wisdom

When you live life without expectations
life takes you on great expeditions

expectations

A Pocket Full of Wisdom

Bernice Angoh

When kindness is your torch
humanity is affected by your touch

touch of *kindness*

A Pocket Full of Wisdom

Love's true home is in the hearts of men
Are you a good landlord?

rent-free lodgings

Self-love is the cup that draws all good things unto itself

magnetic

Every relationship in your life
is a rendezvous with self

self-date

A Pocket Full of Wisdom

Bernice Angoh

Sometimes we attract who we need
in order to unbecome
what we're not

unbecoming you

A Pocket Full of Wisdom

Life is merely the flowering of death

blossoms

You suffer because you desire
You desire because you're running away from pain
You run away from pain because you're afraid of boredom
You're afraid of boredom because you don't want to be alone
You think you're alone because you don't know yourself
You don't know yourself because you shun solitude
But it's in solitude that you'll find yourself
And when you know who you truly are…
You will laugh at it all

existential drama

They taught us to measure time
so that they can steal eternity
from under our noses

time thieves

Everyone in your life
is playing their part
whether disappointing or approving
hurtful or loving
you'll see, someday, it'll make sense
one day you will realize
you're always drawing unto yourself
the most benevolent outcomes

the waking dream

Bernice Angoh

Resilience is the mother of luck

luck

A Pocket Full of Wisdom

Light demands darkness
there is no bypassing, no shortcuts
there is no spirituality without conflict
no beauty without ugliness
no form without chaos
no pleasure without pain
no life without strive

bittersweetness

Their agenda is to have you focused
on achieving and fitting in
rather than
unlearning, healing, growing and living
which all require
stillness, feeling, rebellion and knowledge of self
Once you start to embody all of these
it is harder to fit in

feel

Spirituality is not all about
feeling good
but being able to feel
all range of feelings

let life caress you

Bernice Angoh

You'll begin to live an authentic life
once you have nothing to hide

come out-- of hiding

A Pocket Full of Wisdom

Bernice Angoh

Your love for self will be complete
when you're able to love
the unlovable within yourself

shadow self

A Pocket Full of Wisdom

Bernice Angoh

Pain and suffering
are excavators of sorts
allowing us to feel deeply

keep digging

A Pocket Full of Wisdom

The more married you are
to your darkness
the brighter
you'll shine

say 'I do'

Once you start to heal,
relationships that are not wholesome
or beneficial to your expansion
will begin to fall away

shedding

For new seasons to begin
others must end...
there are other chapters in your book of life
besides the one you're stuck on
and countless books in your Akasha
with marvelous adventures
awaiting you...

let go (read up)

Bernice Angoh

Endings are portals to new worlds

enter.

.

.

boldly

A Pocket Full of Wisdom

If you've ever been on the verge
of a complete meltdown
and frantically tried to call someone
but no one's picking up…
those are the moments you either need
stillness to hear the answer from within
or harness the strength
to pick yourself up

you got it!

There in the hearts of the forgotten,
the hungry
the wounded, the resilient,
I see many familiar faces…
my selves…

i am another you

Bernice Angoh

Somethings in life are just not meant
for us to have control over

acceptance

A Pocket Full of Wisdom

Bernice Angoh

If you don't fix the hurt and damage inside
you will manifest a projection
of all that you must fix and heal
in form of a person
usually, a romantic partner

the mirror effect

A Pocket Full of Wisdom

Change is the most patient teacher
--also the most relentless

yield

It's better to be friends with
someone who is painfully honest
and genuine
than with someone who tries hard
not to hurt people's feelings
and in doing so is never truthful

which friend are you?

Love isn't always a pulling towards
sometimes it is a pushing away

know when

Bernice Angoh

He who fears death
is one who has never fully lived

live

A Pocket Full of Wisdom

No one, absolutely no one can love you
more than you can love yourself
The pain you feel of not finding someone who can
love you unconditionally is self-inflicted
That pain comes from you running away from yourself
from you ignoring your own self…
That pain is your soul grieving
from the realization that you cannot
see that the love you seek can only be created from within
That pain is suppressed love for self
and only you can free yourself
you're your own redeemer
your own salvation
your own sustainer
everything flows from you

you are unconditional love

Bernice Angoh

There is nothing more spiritual than being genuine

be real

A Pocket Full of Wisdom

At times, those who have been through the fires of hell
carry the fire with them
they either become the light they carry and shine bright
or leave a trail of ashes from everyone they have burned

which one are you?

Bernice Angoh

We do not "find ourselves"
we create ourselves
by discovering & exercising our strengths
and in doing so, we bring meaning into our lives

find your strengths

A Pocket Full of Wisdom

Things aren't always as personal
as they feel
sometimes it's just the mind
being its own worst enemy

projecting

Don't be so focused on pleasing others
to the point of betraying yourself

people pleasing

A Pocket Full of Wisdom

All of life is a give and take
nothing is gained until something is gained
and sometimes to gain one has to lose

balance, give & take

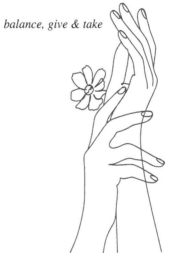

Don't fall into the trap of victimhood
it'll destroy your potential
by robbing you of the power within

move, do, act, correct

Bernice Angoh

Do you like everyone?
no?
in the same way,
not everyone will like you
and that's okay

cure for people pleasers

A Pocket Full of Wisdom

Of the five stages of grief
acceptance is the hardest
because you not only have to embrace the pain
you must also surrender to it
you have to stitch that pain to the hem of your life
and wait till it comes undone-- eventually
pain doesn't go away with time
you just learn to loosen your grip on it.

grief

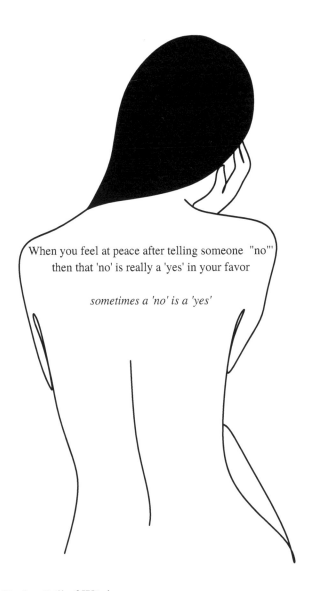

When you feel at peace after telling someone "no"'
then that 'no' is really a 'yes' in your favor

sometimes a 'no' is a 'yes'

Bernice Angoh

To truly enjoy life
one must be a tad foolish
To make good choices
one must embrace failure as a compass
To practice humility
one must learn to laugh at oneself
To gain wisdom
one must accept life's invitation to experiences
To be immortal
one must be a lavish spender of kindness

the magical code of life

A Pocket Full of Wisdom

ABOUT THE AUTHOR

Originally from Cameroon, West Africa,
Bernice Angoh is an award-winning poet, author,
mystic & transformational coach.
She is also an editor & publisher at PAPERHEARTBOOK.

Dubbed "Rumi-woman Incarnate" and "Goddess of love",
her raw, poignant, soul-tugging, shamanic and healing writing
is both alchemical and transcendental.
Ms. Angoh began writing at the ripe young age of 10,
a gift which evolved over time to include themes of
mysticism and metaphysics.

Her work has been featured in several anthologies,
and her articles published both online and in print.
She is a contributing author to very prestigious
literary works including
one of the largest book franchises in the world,
Chicken Soup For The soul.

Unbecoming You, Living in the Flow:
Demystifying manifesting & co-creating a life of ease,
Dear Me: Love letters to my inner child
and *Ananda* are a few of her bestselling books.
Ms. Angoh is currently working on a poetry series
and a children's book series.
Her previous poetry books include *Lemonade street*
and *When a Woman Loves A Man.*

Ms. Angoh spends her time enjoying nature,
dancing, creating & spending time with her loved ones.

AUTHOR, BERNICE ANGOH

All my Links:
https://linktr.ee/iammagic9

Made in the USA
Columbia, SC
31 January 2024

31262742R00070